T0063483

The T-CAR

At Last!
A Simple Vehicle to Fulfill
Your Dreams and Goals.

Dr. Kenneth E. Duffie

Order this book online at www.trafford.com
or (www.KEDuffieDDS.com)
For bulk orders and to contact author:
the_t-carked@cox.net
or email orders@trafford.com

Most Trafford titles are also available at major online book retailers.

Printed in the United States of America.

ISBN: 978-1-4907-2986-2 (sc)
ISBN: 978-1-4907-2988-6 (hc)
ISBN: 978-1-4907-2987-9 (e)

Library of Congress Control Number: 2014904471

Trafford rev. 06/04/2014

 www.trafford.com

North America & international
toll-free: 1 888 232 4444 (USA & Canada)
fax: 812 355 4082

DEDICATION

To the loving memory of Kourtney E. Duffie, my firstborn grandson whose life was interrupted in June of 2007. To my loving sister Vivian Duffie Lance and my very good friend Larry B. Walls, both of whom departed in June of 2013.

May they all rest in peace.
Love always!

Contents

ACKNOWLEDGMENTS

This has been an emotionally ambivalent journey. At times it has been difficult, to say the least, and an uphill struggle. At other times it has been a labor of love and a very gratifying experience of growth. However, during this entire endeavor, I have never been without the support of my family and friends.

I would like to thank my good friends Percy Pierce, Tyrone Stephens, and Don B. Fair for always being there for me in my corner, for believing in me, and for their unrelenting encouragement. I would also like to thank my daughter Karen Duffie for all the professional help she gave me, and not only for helping me with some of my initial proofreading and editing but also for her input with introducing me to the large and complex world of publishing. And finally I would like to thank my loving wife, Delitha, affectionately known as Dee Dee, for all her help in every aspect of this endeavor. For suffering with me, for being my number-one critic, and for being my biggest and most faithful support, always!

AUTHOR'S NOTE

It has been said that *repetition is the mother of learning,* therefore, be aware that the repetition in this booklet is not casual redundancy but is deliberately and intentionally done for the sake of learning and reinforcing many of the main points and quotations deemed worthy of remembering, especially the understanding and functioning of the *T-CAR formula*!

INTRODUCTION

This little book is the result of all the positive thinking and self-help and motivational books that I've read over the years including, most importantly, the Bible. I've been influenced by such authors as James Allen, Maxwell Maltz, Napoleon Hill, David Schwartz, Steve and Sean Covey, Tony Robbins, Joel Osteen, T. D. Jakes, and Joyce Meyer, just to mention a few.

As a result of so much good teaching by so many good authors, I was left feeling pulled in many different directions, always trying to remember who said what, what to do, and when to do it. Although most of what was being taught was good and effective, every author was guilty of just trying to teach their own individual methods, which were very detailed, sometimes overlapping, and too often only taking different roads to reach similar results. Well, this can get to become very confusing, and as you know, confusion often leads to a mental paralysis where you end up accomplishing nothing.

Therefore I began to pray, asking God to give me a solution that would eliminate all the long, detailed procedures, the confusion, and most importantly, the mental paralysis. A solution that would pull all these teachings together into one *short, simple, easy-to-use formula* that could be used to help everyone achieve their dreams and goals and to help you live a more successful, productive, and fulfilling life, and this book is the result of those prayers.

DEFINITION

The T-CAR is a short, simple, easy-to-use *success formula* designed to help you reach your dreams and goals and to help you live a more enjoyable, successful, and productive life.

Just like a car is used to get you from one place to another, from point A to point B, you will be able to use this simple success formula, the T-CAR, to take you from where you are now to where you want to be in every area of your life. The T-CAR will help you with your diet, your financial goals, your attitude, your personal relationships, your spiritual growth, and anything else you are trying to achieve.

OWNER'S MANUAL
THE QUICK START

How the T-CAR Works!

Step 1. Think—Start out each morning by asking yourself this all-important question: What can I do today that will bring me closer to my dreams and goals and make this the best day I ever had? This question is asked intentionally to provoke the mind (your thought factory) to start producing *thoughts*, not just random thoughts but thoughts that line up with your dreams and goals. This myriad of thoughts will start rushing through your mind. Therefore, this question also forces you to focus only on those thoughts that are relevant, supportive, and essential to reaching your goals. It forces you to deliberately think productively and to get focused at the "top" of the day.

Step 2. Choose—of these thoughts racing though your mind, you *must now choose only* the *best thoughts*, those that will ultimately be the *most productive* and *bring you closer* to your dreams and goals.

Step 3. Act—*take action now* based on your *choice of thoughts*, not just mediocre action but *giving it your all* and putting your *best* foot forward. Always putting forth your *best efforts* every day, all day, one day at a time!

Step 4. Results—your results are now assured; they have been determined by the *thoughts you chose* and the *degree of action* you took. It's automatic. Action equals Results—they work together; it's cause and effect. That's why it's important to choose the *most progressive thoughts* and to put forth *your best efforts* to get the *best results!* That's it—steps 1, 2, 3. That's how the brain works: provoke a thought, choose a thought, act on that thought. Those three simple steps will lead you to step 4, which is the ultimate end result. It all starts with a thought. Thoughts become things when acted upon! And as you conceive it in your mind, and by the degree of action you take, you achieve it and get the results of those thoughts acted on. Achieving your dreams and goals is where you ultimately want to be. It's good to have a dream, but it's better to reach your dreams! The T-CAR is the vehicle to take you there. It's short, simple, and effective. By repeating these steps daily, you will get closer to your dreams and goals and eventually achieve them all.

Steps 1 through 4 will be elaborated upon as each letter in the acronym of T-CAR is discussed and explained in more detail to follow.

CHAPTER 1

T

I *think*, **therefore I am!** It all begins with *thinking*! To diet, exercise, write a book, save money, build a relationship, start a career, change careers, or solve a problem—it all begins with thinking. Of course you eventually have to make a *choice*, and inevitably, you have to take *action*, but it all starts with thinking.

The beginning of everything, except creation, begins with a thought. Look around you and everything you see; the iPhone and iPad, cars, airplanes, super fast trains, microwave ovens, blenders, toasters, TVs, radios, air conditioners, skyscrapers, every invention, Broadway plays, Hollywood movies, and everything else you can think of, as the list goes on and on to include all we see around us. Everything—they all began as a thought in someone's mind. Every situation that you're in now or have ever been in was due to your own thoughts. You are *where* you are and you are *what* you are because of your thoughts. The Bible says in Proverbs 23:7 KJV, "For as he thinketh in his heart, so is he," and James Allen added, "as he continues to think, so he remains." If physically we are what we eat, then *mentally* (our personality, our character, and our attitude) we are what we think! So the mind is a thought factory, and a man is what he thinks and continues to think. Paraphrasing Joyce Meyer "as the mind goes so goes the man", the *T* in this formula is for *thinking* or *thoughts.* Everything we do in life starts first as a thought. Thoughts are *things,* or should we say thoughts become *things,* but *things* are always thoughts first. So whatever you want to do or become in life will always first exist as a thought.

So at the start of each day (preferably after prayer or during prayer), ask yourself this question: 'What can I do today that will bring me closer to my dreams and goals and help me to have the best day of my life?' This question will provoke your thinking and help to focus your thoughts on your dreams and goals and toward having the best day of your life as well. If a football team plans to go undefeated and win all sixteen games in a season, then it must win the very first game; they have to start out winning. Use this question to get you focused and thinking on the winning "game plan" for today. It starts with your thoughts! It's the same with your diet, financial goals, or personal relationships; you have to start out winning from the beginning, so be 'in it to win it' the first thing in the morning of everyday and **Think BIG**!

What THOUGHTS started your day?

NOTES

CHAPTER 2

C

Life is a choice. God gives us the freedom of choice, and he expects us to not just choose but to make the *best choices*. The Bible says, "Choose you this day whom you will serve," so we are also expected to make the *right choices*. You should make choices that will give you the greatest and best use of your *time* and *energy and that will bring you closer to your dreams and goals*.

We have a choice in every situation of our lives. Every day our minds are bombarded with a flood of thoughts like water flowing over Niagara Falls. It's like a smorgasbord of thoughts of all varieties, passing before our mind's eye like multiple-colored jellybeans on a conveyor belt. Thousands, if not millions, of thoughts race through our minds competing for our attention, and all day every day, you possess the power at any moment to *choose* to address any thought you desire. All thoughts are not good, and some are more important than others. It's important to choose thoughts that are God-like and empowering. Choose thoughts that advance and support your *plans* and that bring you closer to your *dreams*, your loved ones, others, and closer to *God*. Since life is a choice, then choose thoughts that *motivate* you, choose thoughts that are *loving* and show *kindness*, choose *happiness* every day, choose thoughts that are *challenging* and bring out the *best* in you, choose to be *proactive* and *productive*, and choose thoughts that not only *benefit you* but also *benefit others*! So the *C* in our formula is for *choice*.

Choosing a thought, unfortunately, does not automatically guarantee you the results of that choice. No more than just because you choose to diet, you don't automatically lose weight. While it is absolutely a matter of choice, you *must* follow up that choice with the appropriate *action* to assure yourself of the *results* you want!

What CHOICES did you make?

_____
_____
_____
_____
_____
_____
_____
_____
_____
_____
_____
_____
_____
_____
_____
_____
_____
_____
_____
_____
_____
_____
_____

NOTES

CHAPTER 3

A and R

A is for *action*, and *R* is for *results*, **A** *equals* **R**. In our formula, *A* and *R* are *equal* to each other; they are like "a stamp to a letter, like birds of a feather, they stick together." Sorry I couldn't resist that; I'm from Motown. But *A* and *R* are equal; they are cause and effect. *Action* is cause, and *results* is effect. Every action is a cause, and every result is an effect of that action! But, and this is the *big* but, the "key" to making *anything* work, any program any plan, goal, dream, diet, or any desire you choose, is to take action. Nothing starts by itself, and if you expect to finish, then you have to start, and this includes even your faith!

The Bible says, "Faith without works/ACTION is dead." You have to be a doer, and doers get things done! It takes action to make faith work. And as the body is dead without breath, your dreams and goals are dead without action. God said, "I've come so that you might have life and that you might have it more abundantly." Life is action and action is life! Have you noticed that anything not moving is either dead or being left behind? And unless you *move* from where *you are*, then where *you are* is where *you'll always be*!

It has been said that "Once we decide, our destination is determined." Well, I like to say it a little differently and that is, "Once you decide (on your goal dream, etc.), take action, stay focused and committed, then your destination is *assured*." So as you can see, deciding or choosing is good, but it's not enough by itself; you *must* take action. You can have the best plan (to lose weight or whatever), the biggest and noblest dream (become a multimillionaire and philanthropist), but if you don't take any *action*, if you don't *act*, then you get no results! That's it, plain and simple: no action, no results. That's why I say action and results are equal. If you take little action it equals little results, if you take big action = big results, and of course, no action = no results! That's why so many diets and dreams fail, because of little action or no action at all. That's why A equals R in the T-CAR formula.

So it's all about what you do! The action you take, based on the thoughts you choose, determines the results you get. "Eureka!" That's it, it doesn't get any easier than that; *the action you take based on the thoughts you choose daily determines the results you get.* If you're not getting the results you want, then always look at what actions you're taking. From time to time, you do have to *monitor* and *evaluate* your progress along the way and make changes as needed.

Don't be reluctant to change. Change is a natural part of life, and life is *always* changing, and hence, you should *always be willing* to change for the better. Even the Bible tells us to "be you transformed or changed by the renewing of your minds." You have to start thinking and acting different. So don't be afraid to revise your plans and do things differently.

Even in football during the game, the QB (quarterback) will sense a need to call an "audible" (a quick change in plans) without going into a huddle. Well, life is also like that, where you have to call an audible and make a *quick change* in your plans. If your plans are to go north and you get in the car and proceed south, you'll never arrive at your intended destination unless you make a *quick change* in directions.

Be willing to change if you're not getting the results you desire. If you aren't losing weight, then *change your actions*. If your personal relationships aren't getting any better, then *change your actions*. If your financial goals aren't getting any better, then *change your actions*; if you aren't growing spiritually, then *change your actions*.

No more blame game. The T-CAR formula prevents you from blaming anyone else because it's all about what actions you take—only you, not anyone else. Only what *you do* determines what *you get*! You can only point the proverbial blame finger at yourself. Like Michael Jackson said, "If you want a make a change then start with the man in the mirror!" That's you, okay! It's not about anybody else. Shame on my parents for what I am today, but shame on me if I stay this way! Shame on you if you don't change, and it's never too late to change. Make no mistake about it; thoughts and choices are important and inevitable, but the *ultimate key* to making your dreams or goals come true is the action *you* take, not anyone else!

Think, Choose, Act, and Receive—weight loss   THE T-CAR
Think, Choose, Act, and Receive—financial gain   THE T-CAR
Think, Choose, Act, and Receive—better relationships   THE T-CAR
Think, Choose, Act, and Receive—spiritual growth   THE T-CAR
Think, Choose, Act, and Receive—your dreams   THE T-CAR

It's all good! It starts with *good* thoughts, then *good* choices, and taking *good* action, which ultimately brings *good* results.

This formula works for whatever thoughts you *choose* to apply to it as long as you take action. Besides, we go through this process to achieve whatever we do in life whether we are aware of it or not. We think, we choose, but far too often, we fail to *follow-up* with the appropriate *action*!

But now that you are aware, you just have to choose the *best thoughts* that go along with your dreams and goals and take the *right action* or, that is, the highest degree of action to get the best results you ultimately want. Remember! The *action you take* is an essential ingredient. Make no mistake about it—your thoughts and choices are important, but that's all they are, thoughts and choices, *until you take action*. The moment you take action and stay focused and committed to your destiny, your dreams and goals are assured. But again, remember, the size of that result (i.e., *amount of weight you lose*) is always equal to the *effort*, the size of the action that you put into it!

THINK, CHOOSE, ACT = RESULTS

Think, choose, act, and get the results you want! I can't emphasize this enough. I know it sounds redundant, but just keep repeating this simple little formula to yourself over and over: think, choose, *a*ct, and get the *r*esults I want!

Think, choose, act, and get the results you want! As you continue to repeat this powerful little formula over and over and begin to apply it to your *plans* and *dreams* knowing that it's the size of your action that will *determine* the size of the results you get and then something miraculous will happen, your goals will start to materialize and your dreams will start to come true! This formula is so simple yet so powerful. It's an outward expression of how the brain works, and I strongly believe that the T-CAR was a godsend, an answer to my prayers and hopefully yours. What could be any simpler, any more divine than choosing your thoughts, taking the right action, and getting the results you want? It's as simple as one, two three; the T-CAR!

What ACTION did you take?

_____

_____

_____

_____

_____

_____

_____

_____

_____

_____

_____

_____

_____

_____

_____

_____

_____

_____

_____

_____

_____

_____

_____

What were your RESULTS?

NOTES

Procrastination

Yesterday, I said I would until the time had passed,
And now today, I see my list of never-ending tasks.
"Why so", I ask myself, "did I put off that task at hand?"
For yesterday has added to my ever-growing plans,

Of things I say I will attend, accomplish or provide;
Seems every day I put if off, it multiplies in size!
A simple job if given my devotion for a time;
Would surely have resolved itself and eased my
worried mind.

However, due to circumstance, (as always is the case);
I had no time to spend that day, "I had no time to waste".
For yesterday, I worked on all the tasks I had delayed,
From days before when I would say "I have no time today".

You see, tomorrow's easier to say that I will vow,
To catch up on the overload, and yet . . . I wonder how?
'Tis easier to play the part of victim in this case,
And be the martyr ever-more, "I have no time to waste!"

© Kit McCallum 1999

CHAPTER 4

CAUTION!
Hazards Ahead

a. Procrastination

The first thing to overcome is *procrastination.*

It has been said that the best-laid plans often go astray or never get off the ground. Why? Well, the biggest and most common reason to all of us is procrastination. Procrastination will turn a pregnant opportunity into a hollow possibility. It is a thief; it robs you of the most important asset you possess and cannot replace; it steals your *time*. Procrastination also steals your *dreams* and it steals from all those who stand to benefit from your achievements! Your dreams and goals should be too important to put off or wait for anything else. If you wait, you will never get started, and winning starts with beginning, and to get to the end, you must first begin.

So don't get so busy revising your plans, trying to make them *perfect* before you ever start, trying to distill and analyze every aspect of it. It has been said, 'too much analysis leads to paralysis' and you never get going—just more precious time wasted and people deprived even longer. So don't wait until it's perfect to start; just get started and refine things as you go along. The important thing is to start. Let it be like a snowball rolling down a hill; it starts out small and gets bigger as it goes along. An imperfect plan acted upon is better than a perfect one that never gets activated. The space shuttle uses 75-80 percent of its fuel just to get off the ground and into orbit. True, it's not easy getting started, but once you get going, it does get easier.

Remember, winning starts with beginning! And the journey of a thousand miles starts with the first step. Take that step now! There will always be a reason not to get started, but you have to start in order to finish, and like Nike said, "Just do it," and do it *now*! Did you know that when you spell the word *now* backward it spells *won*? So as soon as you start, you've *won*; you become a winner! If you find yourself using words like *wait, tomorrow, later, next week, sometime, someday,* or *one day,* then you know you're procrastinating. Those are failure words! When it comes to overcoming procrastination the only success word is *now*, right now! So again, unless you move from where you are *now,* then where you are *now* is where you'll always be! Move *now*!

Procrastination

Procrastination is my curse;
It brings me so much sorrow.
'Course I can quit most any time
In fact, I will! Tomorrow!

b. Habits

***Habits*—habits make or break us.** While we may have
many of them, there are only two kinds of habits, good and
bad. It has been said that we are creatures of habit, but we
are not stuck with any habit. Habits are created by repeated
behavior, doing something over and over until that behavior
becomes automatic or habitual. So we can drop or change
any *bad habit* or reinforce any *good habit*.

In attempting to do anything, your habits will automatically
come into play. The good habits will propel you forward, and
the bad habits will hold you back. Procrastination is nothing
but a bad habit. The way you get dressed in the morning,
brush your teeth, or get along with others—these are all
developed habits, good or bad. Thus you have to become
aware of what your present habits are, especially the bad
ones—which ones you'll need to extinguish and which new
ones you'll need to develop. The way you do things *now*,
where you are *now* in life—your weight, your relationships,
your financial situation—is all a result of your choices and
actions you've repeated over and over that have *now* become
habits!

Start using the T-CAR repeatedly for everything you do until
it becomes a good habit! Just ask yourself at the beginning of
every day (I do this after I have my morning prayer), *"What
can I do today to help bring me closer to my dreams and goals
and to make this the best day I've ever had?"* Then, *think* about
the question, *choose* the best thought (or thoughts), start to
take big *action* and get the big *results* you want!

Continue to use the T-CAR repeatedly. Begin to teach this
success formula to your children, especially if they're
teenagers. Who, more than our children, need to have
successful habits? Teach it to them until it becomes a habit,

an automatic way of successfully getting things done. Just think, if you can be instrumental in changing just one person's life, especially if it's one of your children, then you've succeeded big-time! The habitual use of this success formula will teach you and them to be more productive and responsible. Not blaming others but realizing that you are responsible for your thoughts, your choices, your actions, and consequently, your results.

Just think, if habits can automatically work for us and make us successful and we're not, then we must have the wrong habits. You need to develop and employ more successful habits. So get into *good* habits, and let them work for you, not against you!

Who Am I?

I am your constant companion. I am
your greatest helper or heaviest burden.
I will push you onward or drag you down
to failure. I am completely at your command.
Half the things I do, you might as well
turn over to me, and I will be able to do
them quickly and correctly.

I am easily managed—you must merely
be firm with me. *Show* me exactly how you
want something done, and after a few
lessons, I will do it automatically. I am the
servant of all great individuals and, alas, of
all failures as well. Those who are great, I
have made great. Those who are failures,
I have made failures.

I am not a machine, though I work
with all the precision of a machine plus
the intelligence of a human. You may run
me for profit or run me for ruin—it
makes no difference to me.

Take me, train me, be firm with me,
and I will place the world at your feet. Be
easy with me, and I will destroy you.

Who am I?

I am Habit.

Author Unknown

NOTES

NOTES

CHAPTER 5

Traveling Aids

Keys to Get You Started and Tools to Keep You Going!

a. Commitment
b. Prioritize
c. Benefits
d. Sacrifice
e. Focus

Every invention, anything you build or achieve, all requires the right tools. The right tools make any job easier; just ask any brain surgeon, dentist, or mechanic. Listed below are a few of the tools you'll need to help make your dreams and goals come true.

Commitment. This is the *key*! It is a solemn promise to yourself that you're "in it to win it", that you have swallowed the seed of your dream hook, line, and sinker, and that it is growing within you like the center of a volcano; it burns in your soul. It's alive and lives in you like a baby while you go through the labor and birth pains to push your dream through the birth canal, and then it's finally born into the world for all to see! There's no turning back, and you can't abort; you must go full-term and be willing to go over, under, around, or through whatever you have to endure until you give birth to your dreams!

You have to love your dream because love has no limits. It can bear all things; it can endure all things, and nothing can hold you back! So you have to be *sold out, all in,* and *serious as a heart attack.* So fully committed to your dreams that there's no room to ever quit, only commit! When you're committed, you *do* what has to be done; when committed, you *move* what has to be moved, you *act* to make it happen, and what you absolutely won't do is quit! *If you want it, you will find a way!* If you don't, you will find an excuse. So don't ever make *excuses*; make *commitments*! And you only have to be committed for one day at a time.

Prioritize. Giving your dreams and goals the highest priority—that means to want them more than anything else! To want something so bad you can feel it being pumped out of your heart and running through your veins. It's the first thing you think about in the morning, then all through the day, the last thing at night and all through your sleep, then, wake up and start all over again.

Make your dreams and goals more important than anything else. If you're not starting *now*, then your dreams and goals are not important enough to you. If you don't see them as urgent, high priority, or critical to your life, then you're setting yourself up to be a victim of *procrastination.* You will easily put your dreams and goals aside when they're not the highest priority to you! You have to be passionate about pursuing them. It has been said that 'life is in the blood', so literally you feel your dreams flowing through your blood vessels. It's your *life* that you're investing into it. It's your *time*, and time is your most precious procession. When you procrastinate and don't prioritize, what you're saying is that "something else is more important than my dreams and goals" and you're giving that something else a higher priority. You're also saying that this other thing is also more important than you, your loved ones, or whoever stands to benefit from your achievements. So get your priorities in order, and then stay committed.

Benefits. Reaching your dreams and goals will bring rewards. These rewards are very important motivators. Like I just said above, knowing all who stand to benefit from your achievements is also motivational, whether it's just you, your loved ones, or all humanity. This is so important to be aware of because these are the same people who lose out, who will suffer more, and who are further denied when you procrastinate or don't prioritize. Stay mindful that your lack of action hurts not only you but others as well! So always be aware of not just *who* benefits but *what* those benefits are.

What benefits, rewards, or end results do you *associate* with achieving your dreams and goals? See these benefits in your mind, write them down on paper, and post them where you can see them the first thing in the morning and the last thing at night. Allow these benefits to become real to you. See yourself with them. See the weight loss, the fun, the increase in energy, the change in your personality and attitude, that new home you'll buy, the traveling you'll be able to do, college for your children, and the changes you'll bring about into the lives of others as well! Feel the joy and happiness your achievements will bring to you, to your love ones, and to everyone else. What you associate with your achievements is what will motivate you and keep you going. The benefits, the end results, are your "why." It's the reason; it's *why* you're doing what you're doing. Make your benefits clear, and keep them in clear view, in focus! Focus on staying the course, sticking to your plans for just one day at a time as each day brings you closer to those benefits.

Sacrifice. Throughout my life, I've noticed that what most people readily sacrifice more than anything else are their dreams and goals. They become complacent and settle for a life less meaningful and less fulfilling but will continue to work very hard to help other people make their dreams come true. And that is a sad thing, because not only do you and your loved ones lose out, but so does everyone else. Just think, if Thomas Edison had given up on his dream for light, if Alexander Graham Bell had given up on his dream for the telephone, if Henry Ford had given up on his dream for the automobile, the Wright brothers on their dream to fly, or other inventors like George Washington Carver, Jonas Sulk, Walt Disney, Steve Jobs, Bill Gates, Colonel Sanders, and others had given up on their dreams, how different the world would be. Your dreams may not be as big as theirs or have such great humanitarian benefits, but your dreams could be life changing to you, and you could impact the next person to do something great, and so on. Look at the tremendous affect such little things like duct tape, the ballpoint pen, a binary number system, cut and paste, or even popcorn has had on all of us.

The Bible says, "Little is much in God's hand" and "Don't despise the day of small beginnings." In the hands of God, all things are possible, and with a little, he can do a lot. Remember, he doesn't just add to what you have; he multiplies it and blesses a multitude! So don't give up on your dreams, no matter how small they may seem. When you don't reach your highest potential, we all lose.

Nothing worthwhile is ever achieved without sacrifice. Sacrifice is not just a key ingredient in achieving success;

it is a must ingredient! So be willing to give up something you value in order to have something you regard as even more valuable. Sacrifice is the cost you have to pay. Because of the personal and humanitarian benefits you stand to gain, always stay mindful that the *rewards* are greater than the *sacrifice*. Be willing to sacrifice for the *greater good*, for all those who stand to benefit from your sacrifice. Jesus Christ, Mahatma Gandhi, Martin Luther King Jr., and Nelson Mandela—they all made great sacrifices for the benefit of humanity. Many different types of sacrifices will confront you along your journey. There will be lack of sleep, getting up early and staying up late; not being able to eat this or that; taking the stairway and not the elevator, days, weeks, months, maybe even years of delayed gratification; destitution; solitude; being misunderstood; the daily struggle to keep going even though you want to quit; barring the burden of knowing others are depending on you and finding time and energy to go on when your body is ready to collapse; giving up TV or movies; and you may have to work harder and study more. Although I can't name or number all the different kinds of sacrifices you'll have to make, I can only assure you that in order to succeed, you will have to make sacrifices, but the reward is always greater than the sacrifice. Therefore, be willing to sacrifice daily for the greater good!

Focus. Since thoughts become things, tune out all thoughts that are not a part of your plan! Focus only on the plan, and see everything else as a distraction; a thief to steal your dreams!

Focus is the fuel that will keep you going and on the right track! I just can't emphasize enough how important it is to stay focused. Keep your eye on the prize, and actually see yourself achieving your goals! Every day, all day, there will be distractions tempting you away from your goals and dreams. *Resisting* those temptations or distractions is part of making sacrifices and staying focused. Keep your eyes on the prize (the benefits, the end result). Always keep the end results in focus and how important to yourself and others it is to stay on course. Don't be lured away by things that seem more important, interesting, or exciting at the time, but afterward will only leave you disappointed, frustrated, and off-course with more precious time wasted.

To help you stay focused, constantly remind yourself of the benefits, the rewards, the results; your dreams and goals are to all that stand to benefit—this is the *greater good*. Etch in your mind that nothing is more important than to realize your dreams and goals. Remember, while it's good to have a dream, it's better to reach your dream! Focus only on today and take no thought for tomorrow; tomorrow will give birth to its own problems! Be single-minded and stay focused only on the achievements of today and *nothing else*!

F —Eyes forward
O—Oneness in purpose
C —Committed to the plan
U—Unrelenting
S —Steadfast

Focus! And stay that way!

NOTES

CHAPTER 6

Maintenance

Periodically and deliberately take time to monitor and evaluate your progress, your plans, your strategy, and be ready to make changes wherever needed. It's like changing your oil to make your car run better. In today's vernacular, it's like *updating* your iPhone or iPad. As a pilot, I know how important it is to continually make adjustments/changes in flight to arrive at the intended destination. Remember, *shame on my parents for what I am today, but shame on me if I stay this way!* Be willing to change and do things differently. Life is always changing; it's a process of letting go, not being afraid to move out of your comfort zone and to think and act out of the box. Unless you move from where you are now, then where you are now is where you'll always be! Are you where you want to be? If not, then move now! If you don't change, then things (your life) won't change for you!

CHAPTER 7

Start Your Engines!!

From the beginning, know the ending. It sounds like an oxymoron but it's so true. Begin with the end in mind, know what you want right from the beginning, and know why you want it. For example, *what* I wanted from the beginning was a simple success formula that would be short, easy to understand, and use. *Why*, because I believed in my heart that this formula was a god-send and that it would be a tool to help change lives and that it would help make the lives of millions of people including mine happier, more successful, and more fulfilling.

Always make the fulfillment of your dreams and goals so important that there's no way not to start now and no way you could ever quit. Winning starts with beginning. So start and don't be afraid to start and risk failure. Know that falling down is not failure, but failing to get up and start again, is! So never quit; commit. Let that be your resolved unrelenting attitude, to never, never quit and to never, never give up. If you can look up, you can get up, and when you get up, pull others up! So don't quit—*commit*! So don't stall out or stop too soon, for the race is not given to the swift or the strong but to those that endure until the end, and the end is always closer than you think. For one day at a time, always be willing to do a little more, to go a little further, and to try a little harder; *just one more day!* Know that the only way you won't succeed is to quit, and winners never quit, especially when it means so much to so many!

Believe. What you believe is your foundation, the impetus, the wellspring from whence your thoughts emerge. So believe *you can!* Just say you *can*, and you will. You have ATP, All Types of Power, and you have the greatest potential built into your body to do anything, especially something good and worthwhile; it's a gift from God! Therefore, "one day at a time"—that's your focus! Tell yourself that you can do anything for *just one more day,* and then don't just say it, mean it and believe it and then go after it—that's showing your faith by your works, an outward expression that you deeply inside, believe.

Be excited! Pursue your dreams and live your life with passion. Be enthusiastic about your dreams. The root meaning of the word *enthuse* (*in* + *theos*) means "to be in God." Feel God in your life—feel him working in you and with you, make him a part of everything you do and do it for his glory, the greater glory! It's been said that the most powerful weapon on earth is the *soul on fire,* so get fired up! And that enthusiasm will become empowering and contagious. You now have the formula to succeed, the keys to get started, and the tools to keep you going. Therefore get in the T-CAR, the little car that can, can take you to your dream—the "American dream," any dream—and to new heights. So think big, dream big, be willing to sacrifice, stay focused, keep believing, be excited, and don't ever quit on yourself—commit, and I'll see you at the top! Now you're in the driver's seat, jump in the T-CAR and enjoy the journey!

THE BEGINNING!

The T-CAR

Think+**C**hoice+**A**ction=**R**esults

The Simplest and Most Powerful Success Formula

That Works for Anyone and Everyone

Especially *You*!

NOW BEGIN

What can *you* do today that will bring *you* closer to *your* dreams and goals and make this the best day *you* ever had?

The T-CAR!

NOTES